# THE WIND BEYOND THE WALL

# THE WIND BEYOND THE WALL

## POEMS BY JOAN McBREEN

STORY LINE PRESS
1991

ISBN:  0-934257-33-7

Publication of this work is made possible
in part by grants from the
National Endowment for the Arts.

Thanks to the generous support of the
Nicholas Roerich Museum

Book design by Lysa McDowell
Cover photograph by Brendan Lawlor

Published by Story Line Press, Inc.
Three Oaks Farm
Brownsville, OR  97327
U.S.A.

*For Joe, with love.*

## ACKNOWLEDGEMENTS

Acknowledgement is made to the editors of the following publications in which some of these poems first appeared: "The Tuam Herald", "Writing in the West" (The Connacht Tribune), "The Salmon", "Krino", "Cyphers", "Poetry Ireland Review", "New Irish Writing" (The Sunday Tribune), "The Maryland Review" (U.S.), "Visions" (U.S.), "The Cork Yule Book", "The Honest Ulsterman", "The Simon Poetry Anthology", "The Dundalk Poetry Anthology", "Anima", "Riverine", "Limerick Poetry Broaksheet", "W.E.B." (New Irish Writing by Women).

Thanks also to Radio Telefis Eireann who broadcast some of these poems on their programs, "Just a Thought", (Producer, John MacKenna) and on "The Arts Show", (Producer, Seamus Hosey) during 1988.

The author wishes to thank Jane Prendergast who typed the original manuscript of this book and the members of the Galway Writers Workshop for their continuous support.

# CONTENTS

## I

The Gift                                   11

Wild Woodbine                              12

The Glory-Hole                             13

The Neighbour's Daughter                   14

The Green Quilt                            15

The Saints                                 16

Girl with Umbrella                         18

My Grandmother                             20

The Other Woman                            21

Classibawn                                 22

Rabbits                                    23

The Daughter's Song                        25

The Wedding Ring                           26

The Woman and the Igloo                    27

My Space                                   28

The Left Hand                              29

Valkenswaard                               30

My Father                                  31

Woman in Winter                            33

The Broken Swing                           34

Culleenamore                               36

The Wind Beyond the Wall                   37

# II

The Dark 41

River Music 42

The Woman in the Yellow Dress 43

Fall 1987 45

The Woman and the Whitethorn Tree 46

The Hunter's Infidel 47

Primroses in March 48

The Peace-keeper 49

Martha 52

This Moon, These Stars 54

Poem for St. Brigid's Day 56

The Night 57

The Straw Hat 58

The Stones 59

Christmas in Tuam 60

Telephone Call 62

Once 63

Inis Meáin 64

Notes for American Readers 65

About the Author 66

I

## THE GIFT

And two years is it, since my father died?
My family copy me behind my back,
"God help the one who breaks one of those coffee cups".

He carried them downtown in brown paper
and I was twenty-one, walking next to him
on the inside of the narrow Sligo streets.

Two years almost, is it?  We take coffee
from the small brown and white china cups.
Is it my voice breaks?  Am I saying it again?

# WILD WOODBINE

Wild woodbine was beyond my reach
in the thick hedges round Lough Gill.
The heavy scent filled the house for days
when my father brought it in
and it stayed fresh far longer
then meadowsweet.

Because I loved the delicate
pink and white wild rose
he picked it too, cursing the thorns, muttering
"it dies too soon,
you'd be better leaving it alone".

Yet once, when my mother
swept its petals from the floor
I saw him rescue one
and place it carefully
in the small wallet
where he kept her photograph.

# THE GLORY-HOLE

I believed that in the dark place
beneath the stairs, I would be safe
until the game turned sour
and I heard their laughter
after they locked me in

Over and over I am still the one
who crouched down there
long enough to feel
water
seeping down my legs.

I remember nothing of our play
but the sound of everyone running away,
and the empty house echoing my cries
and the heat
in the glory-hole
stifling,
the smell of musty clothes,
old shoes,
the buzz
of a single trapped wasp.

## THE NEIGHBOUR'S DAUGHTER

The neighbour's daughter is painting her toenails
bright red in the afternoon sun

and the room is dark and cool
where her mother is dusting the photograph

of a girl in a white dress on a swing
with her legs near the sky.

Her father stands at the other side
of the gate squinting and averting his eyes.

## THE GREEN QUILT

My mother used to say,
it's the banshee crying on the wind
from the north telling us
who has been lost at sea tonight,
until we would beg for mercy
beneath the green quilt.

At night, with the long curtains drawn,
before we could read or write,
she took us in,
the lamp dark beside the bed
and we lay still listening
to the rain ticking on the roof.

I lie awake now nights
hearing sounds the house makes
and it is her voice I remember
between the sheets,
her voice taking up right
where she had left off.

I feel her heat in the nest
she made for us
under the green quilt.

# THE SAINTS

My father packed his bags and went to sea.
My mother started her knitting again.
My grandmother went to the church to pray
and I began to read "Wuthering Heights",

a story without a happy ending.

At school the nuns told us stories
about "The Little Flower" and "Maria Goretti"
and the bad man who killed her
because she would not do whatever it was
he wanted her to do.

I did not think "The Little Flower"
had a happy time at home
and I felt sorry "Maria Goretti" got killed
but to my mind it was much better
than being a nun.

My mother finished her knitting
and my grandmother kept up the prayers.
When my father came home from sea
I asked him what he thought
about "Maria Goretti" and "The Little Flower"

He said he had never been too sure himself.

When my mother found me weeping
over "Wuthering Heights"
she told my grandmother to buy me a copy
of "The Lives of the Saints".

My father rolled a cigarette
and looked at me.

I looked at him.

## GIRL WITH UMBRELLA

The passersby on the street turned
as you whirled it around
over your head,
imagined yourself a proper lady,
umbrella sky-high, wide open, coloured
yellow with white dancing bears.

In sunlight, plastic basket perched
on your arm, small hand in mine,
your smile trusted the gathering dusk.
A mackerel sky, smell of lilacs
and I was caught, startled,

a child crouched under a dark umbrella,
close to a woman whose body
sheltered my body, both of us silent,
afraid of something
we dared not name.

I wish I could reach that woman now
but I fear her visits to me
like a ghost in the night,
I fear her voice
whispering to me
like rain through trees.

And yet, on you danced my lady,
my girl with the yellow umbrella,
while I remembered
how it was to lie awake in the dark
afraid of even
the curtains' sudden movement.

# MY GRANDMOTHER

My grandmother wore a black coat
for my grandfather's funeral.
I believed she always wore it
until I saw her fast asleep
on the iron bed in the attic,
her mouth wide open,
a Baby Power in her hand
the coat on the floor.

Everyone was afraid of her,
even the priests.
On freezing winter mornings
she and I would walk
up the empty town
early for seven Mass
and she would beat
on the closed church doors with her stick.

Black hat, black coat, black stick,
she bewildered me, except on Fridays,
when she would take me
to collect her pension,
afterwards giving me one and sixpence
and buying beige nylons for herself.

## THE OTHER WOMAN

Hand-washing in the kitchen
turning to watch my child,

I was a child

in another kitchen
watching
a woman weeping
into her washing

her cigarette ash
lengthening and dropping
unchecked on the clothes.

## CLASSIBAWN

We tied ropes to poles on the street,
and the length of the swing
was the length of the rope.
We drew hopscotch squares there too,
and swore at the meat factory girls
who let water drip from tin buckets
spoiling the chalky game.
We were sent on walks to the Holy Well
because it used to take us ages
and my mother thought the air
and the prayers good for us.
Then one summer my father hired a Ford car
and drove us to Mullaghmore
where I saw Classibawn for the first time.
After that nothing was the same.

## RABBITS

Waiting in the heat
near the butcher's door
she made circles
with the toes of her shoes
in the sawdust.

Rhododendrons
stood in jam jars
beside lamb chops
and pictures of "Our Lady Queen of Peace"
and the "Mother of Sorrows".

On Saturdays
the butcher sold skinned rabbits
for half-a-crown
and her mother told the shop
how much her children liked rabbit stew.

When rabbits dart
among rhododendrons
it is Saturday again
and she has pressed
herself back
between the sides of beef.

She is watching her mother
count her change
over and over
and she is looking
down at the sawdust
on her shoes.

# THE DAUGHTER'S SONG

When I knew my mother well
she wore high purple shoes

when I knew my mother well
she wore delicate blue dresses

when I knew my mother well
she wore good white cardigans in bed

when I knew my mother well
she combed her tangled brown hair

when I knew my mother well,

when I knew my mother.

## THE WEDDING RING

In my sleep
I search in deep woods;
I am with a woman whose fingers
reach deeply into the earth.

She wears no wedding ring
for she has lost it in the undergrowth.
Her other children have climbed trees
and are throwing scaldings from their nests.

As thunder mounts behind us,
trucks of cattle roar past,
their faces pressed close
to slats for air.

I see my mother, her hands
in wet dirt, searching,
searching for her ring among pine needles
and the blood of young birds.

## THE WOMAN AND THE IGLOO

My time, she said, has never been my own.
I have so much to do
and do again tomorrow.

Between all of you
I am exhausted, she said,
I will take time off and go away.

So she built an igloo in her head
and found it cold
but private.

She often goes there now
*but still hears the lean wolves howling*
far across the tundra.

## MY SPACE

is somewhere
under our waking
from nights' oblivion,
small bodies diving
for the warm space

between us,

under black crumbs
spilt milk,
mounds of sheets,
or hanging in silence

between me,

the telephone receiver
and my tone deaf
mother.

## THE LEFT HAND

The children
paint their mothers
on newsprint sheets.
All the bright
colours are gone so quickly.

Sitting next to you
the skin on my hands
is streaked black
from the paint on the brush
in your left hand.

The children laugh
at the strange blackness
on your page and point
it out to the women
who wait near the door,
chatting in the sun.

The room is empty now
except for me and you
and your black mother
picture, but
I'm touching your right hand,
wiping your face.

## VALKENSWAARD

Poppies and corn flowers lit
the yellow fields near Valkenswaard
and I felt my child's skin warm
under my fingers as he slept

in the crook of my arms
and the shadows stretched
across the brown wooden floor
under his white bed

when I shook sand
from his scuffed shoes
and heard the whisper of his breath
in the dark room

before moths were drawn
to the candle flaming
over the beer and the bread
on the platter between us

and we crept to bed almost
without remembering
to put his small blue flowers
in the stone water jug on his window sill.

## MY FATHER

My father
was a lonely man
whose fifty years
at sea
had left
no deeper blue
in his eyes.

Once in spring
at Lissadell
he picked bluebells
for my mother
and his eyes
looked different.

He fought
death
a frightened man,
hauled
to unknown rocks
from an ocean
he could
not navigate.

I wonder nights now
what lonely bay
he sails in
and does he
quote his lines of Yeats
and smoke his pipe
and drink the whiskey
for the pain.

## WOMAN IN WINTER

I am a woman in my green kitchen, in winter.

When you come in from the street,
do you see how elegantly
my table is set,
how the chrysanthemums blaze
in the fine glass vase
on the window sill?

I am sitting here waiting
for you to stop talking
about last night's storms.

My apron is hanging
on the back of the chair,
my hands are resting
on the table but
at any moment,
they might lift that vase
and hurl in onto
the brown tiled floor.

## THE BROKEN SWING

Come with me
through the rusting gates
from the streets of the town
into this high-walled garden
and move ankle deep in bluebells
under the beech trees
where the bickering crows
nest high.

Come through the storm door
to the shadows of the house
and when your eyes grow used to the dim light
step over the old papers, the clothes
piled up on the chairs and draw close
to the black and white photograph
of your mother.  Be quiet
and you might even hear the piano played.

Show me the bedroom where you slept,
your toys still on the floor.
Shake the dust from the books
you had forgotten about
and I will follow you then
to the garden with the broken swing.

Mend it quickly and bring
your children here.

Take them in from the town
to pick bluebells in the garden.
Stay near the house with the shuttered windows
from where you first saw the stars.

## CULLEENAMORE

I wish that before we left that place
I had told you the story
of how the Atlantic salt-waters'
taste in my mouth
leaves me loneliest.

It was that kind of Sunday afternoon
in Culleenamore,
a wind through the bent grass and sandhills
making me want to begin
a history of my past,
every chapter unfolding

pictures of a man
lying under a hawthorn, reading,
his jacket bundled into a pillow,
a woman straining her ears
hard to hear the voices
of a boy and his sisters

disappearing into the perilous water.

# THE WIND BEYOND THE WALL

The wind beyond the high wall
at the back of our house
contained itself there,
when barefoot, on the cold bedroom floor
I pressed my face against the glass.

Curtains billowed back created
swaying shadows in the small room.
The night was another world
and I was safe, apart
from the wind beyond the wall.

The lamp before the Sacred Heart glowed,
coals hissed in the grate
and on days missed from school
the hands of the clock on the mantelpiece
seemed scarcely to move at all.

On the small round table
she set cups, plates, new bread.
Mice scuttled in the skirting
when she softly dusted the photograph
of the man in uniform.

In dreams I see his face, recognize
his penetrating gaze
and she and I are back in that house
wanting something beyond
my touch, beyond hers.

II

## THE DARK

I need to believe your door opens
at my slightest touch
and that I can still close it
quickly behind me,
shutting out December.

I hold you against me,
my bones soft
since they touched you.

Keep me well back from the window,
for once I climbed up
and looked down to the street.

If ever you left me,
my fall would take me
past window after window.

I would tumble into the dark,
but my heart would remain
in your room,
huddled in a secret corner.

# RIVER MUSIC

Warm enough to wear my purple dress
with white polka dots,
my arms and your arms
brown and bare,
                    and a small wind
blowing in over the river
lifting your hair and my hair
a little.

People passing on the street
keeping us from shouting
at one another.

I have dreamed of you since then,
kneeling beside the river
trying to fill my bucket
and I am holding on to you.

I have dreamed of you
hauling it heavily from the water
and turning from me,
letting it slip in again,
                    and a small wind
blowing over the river
lifting your hair and my hair
a little.

# THE WOMAN IN THE YELLOW DRESS

There was nobody in the field,
so she went in
through the gate
in her yellow dress,
her stomach in a knot,
and she lay down
in the wet grass, the first
to leave the shape
of a body there.

She opened her dress
because there was nobody
to see her and she slept
while the whole of the summer
hummed around her
and she dreamed
of no wretched weather.

Waking, she shook her hair free
from the thick pins that tightened
it in a coil
at the back of her neck
and for a time
the grass stopped growing
where she lay, and she forgot
his voice, his arms, until

he approached her
with wolves on his shoulders.
She braided her hair
and buttoned her dress.

Taking the wolves from him
into her arms she followed
him out through the gate
with her heart full of grey snow.

## FALL 1987

Autumn crawls into the house
where we go on reading,
lying on the bed, chain smoking,
tired working at trying to return
to where we were.

We reach
for one another's hands,
holding on until the fingers whiten,
changing us into skeletons.

We are the worse for wear, old ghost.
Remember summer?  Nothing caught fire.

## THE WOMAN AND THE WHITETHORN TREE

It blossoms during the night,
whitely haunting the black air.

You have only to wait, it will be there
when swallows tilt low
over fields left
at the bare beginning of winter.

An evil thing, it will find you
if you are a woman searching
for mushrooms, finding instead
a cave in the woods.

A woman like this remembers others
shrieking when these branches
were first carried in.

She is not their kind.
She wears silk in her cave, her arms
naked and shining she eats red berries
and weaves garlands of whitethorn for her hair.

# THE HUNTER'S INFIDEL

Forsythia blossoms near the lair
where the wolves sleep,
while in the forest
the hunter builds his fire.

The woman moans
between white sheets and cries aloud
for a wolf is snarling
at her door.

Far from women's cries and women's arms
the hunter kills
the first wild creatures to appear
in morning shadows.

The woman rises, coils her hair
and tends the stove
humming new music
to herself.

The hunter crosses the fields
and heads for home.
His dark foot-prints stretch
steadily behind him in the snow.

## PRIMROSES IN MARCH

I placed them in the earthenware jug, asking,
"what do they remind you of?"
The question hung in the air
while I floated for a moment on a breeze
that crossed his face.

I thought of Sligo lanes and primroses
clawed from moss beneath trees,
taking them home
to my mother, filling her lap
with damp stems, their broken heads.

Earlier that day
I pulled these frail ones
to ease a particular hunger of my own,
later wishing I had left them
where they had grown.

From that bleak headland
I took primroses for free,
the mist from Lough Corrib
biting to the bone
through the thin lilac dress I wore.

March hailstones jittered
against the window pane
and we talked on lightly
as if the sun still shone
on the fragile flowers between us.

# THE PEACE-KEEPER

*Dedicated to the memory of Aonghus Murphy, killed on
active service with the Unifil troops in the Lebanon, August 1986.*

The soldier's
dark-haired girl
had never seen

the scorching
Lebanon
sun

beat
its furious heat
on the yellow hills.

She did not hear
the screech
or flap

of frightened birds
or see them
fly

senseless
in the smoke-filled
sky.

She did not hear
the soldiers
there

curse and swear
before
they filled

the humid foreign
air
with cries.

And when
her peace-keeper's body
came home

no coolin airs
or purple-heathered
August haze

over brown
midland bogs
softened
the treachery.

No Army dirge,
or flags at half-mast
in silent
towns,

no sympathy,
or priest's gentle words
could change

her lament to lullaby,
or keen
him

ever from the damp
sea-salted
Galway soil.

## MARTHA

Martha, finding shade beneath
laburnums, remembered the market,
how women laughed at her extravagance,
a pound of costly perfume,
pure oils, best grain
for bread.

Lazarus, her brother
who entered death,
walked once more between trees
and she caught his eyes in detail
and delight.

Martha, weaving in silence, grew cold.

She who trembled when His name, their guest,
"The Nazarene" was first raised
on the wind around Jerusalem,
found she asked
for more.

She who built fires, baked bread,
uncovered their good ware,
filled the house with light
and sweet flowers, now
drew her thin cloak about her
and wept.

Even the birds were still.  Martha
caught the scent of perfume
in the garden as evening
turned to night.

The Master was with her sister, Mary.

She was wiping His feet
with her hair.

## THIS MOON, THESE STARS

Something is changing.
There is a September stillness in the garden.

We have woken in this bed for years.
You have followed me into my poems,
my dreams, my past, to places I scarcely
know of myself.

I called one evening
from our back doorstep. "Look," I said,
"look at this moon." We stood there
in silence, not touching, not knowing
what to say.

We have been together many days, many nights.
These stars have come out
over us again and again.

Here is the life we are living,
not on a windswept beach, not in vast
city streets, not in a strange country
but here, where we have chosen to be.

I look at myself in the glass, at the woman
I am.

I think of our days, our years running on
into each other.

What will we say,
what will we know.
Separate, together,
will we find the right way, the dream
neither of us can explain.

I pull the living room curtains together.
The garden is around us,
still above us are the stars,
light and indestructible.

# POEM FOR ST. BRIGID'S DAY

## I

Children gather rushes,
wind whistles through their fingers,
rain blurs their vision;
all evening they will weave
and interweave crosses,
the history of Brigid's love.

## II

It is early morning.  A chieftain
slowly lifts his head, sees a woman enter
bearing armfuls of green spokes.
Her face floats
all day about him, her body's outline
vague.

He woke twice that night,
wandered to the window
tired with darkness,
unaware what had bound them
together; spring, perhaps,
the green stems,

her breath warm
on his face or their two shadows
caught in branches outside
like fish in a net.

## THE NIGHT

When the light
filtered
through

and the half slept
night was
over

my silence
survived
you.

The day had
its usual
order.

Downstairs
the door banged hard
after you

and I lifted
my pile of clothes
from the floor.

## THE STRAW HAT

Some things insist on becoming lost,
like the be-ribboned straw hat
the girl waved over the bridge
to me.

How ridiculous it looked,
floating on the water
between two swans
who were coaxing
one another to love.

Although I tried to reach it,
it was swept away.
"Sit still in the boat, you fool,"
she called, "sit still
or you'll fall into the river."

## THE STONES

What's it to me now
that you once came here
in the middle of summer,
in a deluge.

On a day when I would have believed
anything, you told me
the four stones you found
represented the chambers of your heart.

Having since brought me
to the pebble-beach,
is it now so wrong
to insist that these stones
have hardened into odd shapes
with rough edges,
that some have holes
the water seeps through?

# CHRISTMAS IN TUAM

The famished sheep huddle
near low stone walls,
in watery fields on the Milltown road.

In the town, coloured bulbs
are hanging in rows
across the narrow streets.

Near the square, scavenged fir-trees
and scarce branches
of barely-berried holly

lean like desolate drunkards
against
the library walls.

Men with perished hands
pass small change
from half-wet paper notes,

shoving
the bartered bargains
in the boots of cars.

Even on Christmas Eve
when the town is lit up
early

and distracted women
shopping late
have joined brutish men
in pubs,

I will still be searching
for new words
to believe again in
the reason for it all.

# TELEPHONE CALL

Today a friend called
from a great distance and asked me
was I happy.

It was twilight in November
and the face I looked at
in the mirror

was the face of a child
who had woken in the night
to the sound of crying.

It was the face of a girl
who had turned away from a man
and was suddenly afraid of the dark.

It was the face of a woman
who stood alone in a white room
holding back her hair with her hands.

I told the friend who called
I was quite happy but
I whispered it in one breath.

## ONCE

Today I am alone in a barren place
in October.
Swans are on a small lake
between two hills
and it is cold.
Over my right shoulder
I see the field
where our bodies once crushed
ox-eyed daisies
and your voice was in my hair.

## INIS MEÁIN

Who, seeing me, knows I walked
through fields of corn
and, with you, once heard
the lost curlew mourn
when even north winds were delicate;
I reach this place over and over,
retrace my steps from Cill Cheannach
to Dun Chonchuir despite the roughness of stone.

For I need the sound the high wind makes
in the dry grass, the old and low
notes of island melody, sung at night
when summer is almost ended; and the silence,
full as rains falling after Sunday Mass
on the fringes of island women's shawls.

# NOTES FOR AMERICAN READERS

In the poem, "My Grandmother" on page 10:
a Baby Power refers to a small bottle containing two measures of Power's Irish whiskey.

"Classibawn" on page 12:
is from the Irish, "caisleán bán" which means "bright castle". It is the name given to a castle residence situated in Mullaghmore, County Sligo.

In "The Peace-keeper" on page 37:
the word "coolin", from the Irish "An Cúilfhionn" means "fair-haired woman" and is known in Ireland as an enduring traditional love song.

St. Brigid in "Poem for St. Brigid's Day" , page 44:
is the patroness of Ireland; called in Irish "Muire na nGael" or "Mary of the Gaels". Her Feast day falls on February 1st and is traditionally observed in Ireland by the making of rush crosses.

"Inis Meáin", page 52:
is the middle island of the three Aran Islands situated off the coast of County Galway, Ireland.

Cill Cheannach refers to the monastic remains of a church on the island. Tradition identifies Cill Cheannach, (Kilcanagh), with St. Gregory who gives his name to the Sound between the islands.

Dún Chonchuir is the largest noble fort remains on the islands of Aran. Also called "Dún Conor".

## ABOUT THE AUTHOR

From Sligo, Ireland, Joan McBreen now lives in Tuam, County Galway with her husband and six children. She trained as a Primary Teacher in Dublin and taught for many years.

She has been published in every poetry magazine in Ireland and broadcast on Radio Eireann and her poems are now beginning to appear in North American journals and magazines. Her work has also appeared in several newspapers and she has given readings all over Ireland.

1713